Dedication

To my Abuela and my children

Guided PATH

The Journey from Brokenness to Benevolence

MARISOL SANCHEZ

WITH LISA WALLS

Guided Path
From Brokenness to Benevolence
© 2021 by Marisol Sanchez

Printed in the United States of America

Paperback ISBN-13: 978-1-7358303-7-7
Ebook ISBN-13: 978-1-7370002-0-4

Table of Contents

Foreword

My name is Bobbie Holder. I initially met Marisol Sanchez and learned about Guided Path from a friend. After meeting Marisol and hearing her extraordinary story and all she has overcome, I decided to volunteer at Guided Path. I sensed there was something very special about her and wanted to know more.

This book is important because, despite the difficult obstacles one faces in life, it restores the faith that there are still good and caring people that want to help others. These kind individuals will find a way to offer aid and comfort when others may merely not care; or do not want or chose to put forth the effort. Reading this book will undeniably inspire you to not only feel something, but be motivated to take a look at yourself and think, "What can I do and how can I contribute?"

On a daily basis, I watch Marisol help people. No matter what their needs may be, the answer is not ever no. Perhaps it is not always yes at that particular moment, but never just no. Marisol has helped me believe that genuine, sincere and considerate people still exist that want to help others without asking for anything in return.

When Marisol told me that she was writing a book, my thoughts were that there is no better way for her to share her story with others about what she has gone through and display her big-heartedness of sharing and giving hope to others. I feel that this book will open the eyes of all who read it, as well as demonstrate the fact that most often people end up homeless, jobless, or suffer misfortune through no fault of their own.

When you open this remarkable book, from the first page to the last, your heart, your spirit, and your mind will be touched in a way that you will feel the need to help and give in whatever way you can to change your community for the better.

I cannot put into words the effect that Marisol Sanchez and Guided Path have had on me. This book will do the same for you.

Bobbie Holder

Introduction

I love helping people. When people are treated with compassion and dignity, they change. If you've seen it, you know how powerful it can be.

When people are hurting, they speak softly or not at all. Their faces are drawn, and they look down a lot. You can tell that they're struggling with feelings of shame, regret, fear, and worthlessness. Treat someone like that with just a little compassion and dignity, talk to them like the human being that they are, and their head lifts, their eyes brighten. They want more, so they start showing you how they feel. They start sharing their story. As you interact with them, you can see their countenance change. You can literally see their soul lifting behind their eyes.

Our communities are full of people who are hurting, in crisis, so overwhelmed that they're unable to think through everyday problems. In a post-COVID world, people who have never suffered job loss are experiencing homelessness for the first time. People feel cut off from the family and friends that they didn't realize were keeping them buoyant and moving forward through life's problems. They are discovering that the counsel they've received in the past either doesn't apply now or fails to account for the adaptations that are needed to manage our fast-paced lives, our socially-distant culture, and the relational desert onto which so many have emerged.

My name is Marisol Sanchez. As a social worker and advocate, I have interviewed and worked with countless individuals and families over the years. I have heard about the best and the worst that humanity has to offer. As the founder and director of the fastest-growing non-profit in the Tampa Bay area, I've determined that we must connect to each other, share honestly and openly about ways in which we each can conquer our hurts and fears, and move into action to help the afflicted. Then, our communities— and our world—will change.

My hope is that you will recognize your own exceptional value and worth in this change process. No matter who you are, where you're from, or what you've experienced, there is a calling in your life. Your job is to find out what it is and fulfill it. I hope that my story can encourage you to break through whatever is holding you back to become the self-actualized, compassionate, giving person that you are. I want you to know that there is a place you can go where you are needed, and where you will never be turned away.

Chapter 1

Silent Suffering

We can no longer ignore the truth: the people in our communities are hurting.

You know Richard. You've seen him riding his bike along Hwy 19, backpack filled to the brim. He's a young guy, a little scruffy-looking now, but you can see beneath the overgrown beard and the shaggy hair that he's a rather handsome man in his late twenties. He's clear-eyed, smiles easily, and has a gentlemanly manner for someone so young.

What you don't know about Richard is that he lives in a tent in the woods behind a strip mall. Everything he owns is in that backpack. Richard comes by from time to time and asks us if we have any food. We pack up a bag for him, present the bag with all the graciousness we can muster, only to watch him slowly, apologetically, pull out item after item and hand it back because he has no way to cook rice, or because large jars of spaghetti sauce might break in his backpack.

You probably haven't met Carla. She's a single mom who is running from an abusive ex-husband. She has her 13-year-old son, Tyler, with her. She left when her husband started taking his anger out on him. Her car is packed to the brim with baskets and blankets with only just enough room for her and Tyler to sleep at night. She has no money and can't find a permanent job, but her biggest worry is that, without an address, Tyler can't go to school.

She came to us and we made some calls and found a church that would give her a gas card so she can continue to look for work. But, until she finds a job or a local family to help, she's stuck. You might not know that women's shelters won't house mothers with teenage boys. Teenage boys are too much of a liability, they say.

I know you've run into Glen. He lives in your neighborhood. He's the one who wakes you up on Saturday morning mowing his lawn. But you don't really mind because his yard is the best kept yard on the street and Glen is a really nice guy.

What you don't know is that a few months ago, Glen lost his job. His wife has had some medical issues that ate through their small savings and they've barely been making it week-to-week. But Glen is hard-working and has a great resume, so he was sure he'd find something quickly. In the meantime, he did some day labor and, to get through, took out some payday loans. But the day labor dried up. Companies aren't hiring guys in his field right now. The payday loan cycle has torn apart their budget and they won't make it another month. Soon they will have no car, no home, and his wife cries herself to sleep every night because she knows Glen is trying, but they just can't see a way out.

I meet these people every day. You know many of them. You pass them at work, at the store, and have friendly chats when you go to your mailbox. But we don't really *know* our neighbors, do we? We don't know who is being physically or emotionally abused. We don't know who just emptied their bank account paying the power bill with no hope of having enough to pay rent. We don't know whose child is anemic because their family's food stamp allotment is only a fraction of what it takes to buy healthy food. We don't know who is a recovering addict and who needs emotional and practical support because they've never successfully adulted.

I'm sure that if you went out into your community, you would quickly find the people who are struggling. So many want and need help that, if you just asked them, they would pour out their needs to you in the hope that you might have an answer for them. But then what? What can you do? You're only one person. You have your own challenges. You've spent time and money investing in your education, your growth, and your business. Every day, the Richards and the Carlas tug at your heart and you wish you could help--but there isn't a whole lot left.

I know that dilemma well. I was that mom who cried herself to sleep at night because I was afraid that the man who was beating me would harm my children. I was the homeless mom with a decent resume but who couldn't seem to get a job that paid enough to put a roof over my head. Like you, I found myself looking around saying, "I know I've got it tough, but there are people who are worse off than me, and I have to help." I was a woman who, after so many years of my own struggle, decided to do something about the hurting people in our community. I didn't know how, but I did know one thing: I have no money, but I have faith.

I did know one thing: I have no money, but I have faith.

My name is Marisol Sanchez, and I am here to share with you how we can come together and make a real difference. My non-profit helps thousands of people with life-changing services every year. For enterprising minds in our community, the opportunity to grow and strengthen our businesses, families, and local services while making a difference in our community has never been more important.

Please join me as I share my story and my vision, and we can embark on the mission to help those in need together. Whether you're someone who has a heart to help, has needed help, or just wants to find more purpose in your own life, you are invited to join us on our journey into awakening, growing, facing adversity, and stepping out in faith to build back our communities.

People today are concerned with the bottom line. I am, too. My own entrepreneurial spirit is tethered to the reality of operations and funding. This book will present you with the inspiration and the encouragement that will guide you to powerfully address current issues in your community. I know the need is real. I've lived it. No matter where you're from or what your journey has been, you can make a difference that impacts generations. Now, let's get going!

Chapter 2

The Breaking

Love begins at home
—Mother Teresa

Born and raised on the west side of Chicago, I am a reflection of my roots. The area where I grew up, Humboldt Park, has one of the nicest parks in the city—a large patch of green in the center of miles of concrete. The neighborhood is full of life. Immigrants from Puerto Rico, like my family, built a vibrant community there.

The Pentecostal church my family attended was our community inside the community. The church is where my mom met my stepfather, who has been my dad since before I can remember. My stepfather adopted me and my three older sisters as if we were his own. The church was our support system and our extended family. It was our protection from the world. It was where my parents could confidently raise us to be successful young women of good character.

And, we were. I was an honor roll student and spelling bee winner. I especially loved social studies and history, but I achieved straight-As in all my subjects. And I loved music. I couldn't wait to start playing the violin. My sisters and I had love and support from within and without. We were grateful. We were happy.

But we were also a family full of young girls. And young girls in our neighborhood were the sugar water that young, passionate men hovered over like hummingbirds.

In our church, we were taught and encouraged to study and follow God's will for our lives. His will is to prosper us and not to harm us. His will for us is that we stay in relationship with Him as we seek out relationships of our own. So, while boys and girls might meet and fall in love, there are rules. Families come together and support young people falling in love. They engage with each other. We stay in relationship with each other. But sometimes, when rules are broken, the cracks creep up and around a family and expose the weaknesses and the struggles within.

My middle sister fell madly, deeply in love with a young man. There were many young men in our community, in our church, of whom my parents approved. Unfortunately for our family, my sister's choice was not one of these young men. My parents struggled with her choice. They just couldn't approve. Not him. Anyone but him. My sister struggled against my parents. She was in love. With him. Only him. Something had to give.

When my middle sister ran away at seventeen to be with the young man she loved, she unknowingly created a cascade of reactions that led to fractures in my family and the breaking apart of my own life.

After she left, my mother was not the same. A stay-at-home mom, her family was her world. She didn't speak English, so she was isolated to home and church life. She had struggled with depression before, but the breaking off of a piece of her heart—one of her daughters—was devastating. She went into a tailspin of emotions, resulting in a nervous breakdown.

I was young and able to escape to school and church. My mother struggled to regain her emotional footing, but it was no use. My sister was gone. And my next older sister and I were a daily reminder of her loss. As the youngest, I became a bit of a scapegoat.

"Marisol, all this is your fault."

"*Mamá,* what are you talking about?"

"It was you, Marisol. She left because of you. She was tired of taking care of you. She didn't want to babysit you. You are still so needy. She got tired of helping with you."

"*Mamá,* please don't say that. It wasn't my fault!"

"It was, Marisol. She would have stayed. She wouldn't have chased that boy if she didn't want to get away from watching you."

But I was growing up quickly. At fourteen, I looked much older, and I was experiencing my own first love. Thankfully, Frankie was someone my family approved of. His family went to church with ours and was close friends with our family. He and I had grown up together and we were a natural fit. He was already eighteen, so he would have to wait four years to marry me. But that was okay. He was working in his family business. We had time. And we had a promising future.

My high school days started a wonderful new chapter. I was finally able to take up the violin. Frankie drove me to school each day. He would come over and visit with us on Sundays for our family dinner. He worked with his family of jockeys and trainers racing thoroughbreds at the track.

Frankie worked hard to prepare for our future together. When his family had an opportunity to expand their business into St. Louis, they tapped Frankie for the job. Still fourteen, I was far too young to get married, but my mother decided to take matters into her own hands. In her mind, I was still the daughter who drove my sister away. I was a painful reminder to have around, and she saw an opportunity to alleviate some of her pain.

"Well, then, it's settled, Frankie. You're taking Marisol with you to St. Louis."

"But Marisol and I can't be married for almost four more years. I'm not sure that's a good idea."

"If I say it's okay, then it's okay. I give you both my consent."

"But *Mamá!* I'm still in school! I don't want to be separated from Frankie, but I have to stay here to finish school, at least!"

"No, you don't. You need to go with him. He's going to be your husband someday. Why not start now?"

"Because, *Mamá,* I'm only fourteen! I'm not ready."

I looked at my stepdad, the man who had been there for me since I toddled on the floor. He came from a loving, kind family full of compassionate people. His mother, my *abuela,* was one of my favorite people in the world. What would they think of me living with Frankie?

But my dad only looked at the floor, like a man beaten down. Managing a wife whose bi-polar symptoms were making themselves more apparent each day, he clearly didn't see a way out—for me, or for him.

My mother turned to Frankie. "Then it's decided. Take care of her and make sure she finishes school."

Life in St. Louis was surreal. It was 1986, and I was fourteen and playing house. Frankie and I had our first child when I was fifteen. After a year in St. Louis, we moved back to Chicago and Frankie drove back and forth from St. Louis to Chicago for work. Our second child, a girl this time, arrived when I was sixteen. The next year, my mother was able to officially sign the papers so our marriage could be legal.

Meanwhile, Frankie was moving up in the world. He went from galloper to stall cleaner and finally to assistant trainer. But, while his career was taking off, our relationship was faltering.

I cooked and cleaned and took care of my two children the best I knew how. Frankie was in St. Louis often. I stayed with Frankie's mom. She did her best to guide me. She taught me how to feed and bathe a baby. She helped me understand what to expect as they became toddlers. But, with Frankie gone so often, every day was becoming a lonely battle. I understood how my mother's sense of isolation exacerbated her emotional and mental illness. With my mother and sisters facing their own challenges, I had no one but Frankie's mom.

For five years, Frankie and I lived as husband and wife. Somewhere in the middle of that time, our relationship devolved into something more like brother and sister. And, there was another issue. Frankie was moving up in the thoroughbred community and was re-evaluating his choice of me.

"I can't take you with me, Marisol."

"But, Frankie, I think wives are expected to come to this event."

"I don't think you'd get along with the people. They're not like you."

"What do you mean? You seem to get along with them fine."

"Well, I'm different. I know how to act around them. You're from a different kind of background."

"Seriously? Frankie, we're from the same neighborhood!"

"I know, but I've been around these people my whole life. I understand them. You just don't fit into this world."

"But, Frankie—"

"Marisol, stop!" Frankie snapped. "You don't get it. You're just too ghetto."

I stared at Frankie. If I was too "ghetto" for him to include me in his life, if being smart, capable, working hard, and trying my best wasn't enough, then I was stuck. I couldn't change who I was or where I was from. It had been five years, and it was clear to both of us that our relationship was over. I moved out.

I went and got an apartment through public assistance. Frankie would visit the kids occasionally, but they wouldn't go to stay with him. I was alone with two young children in a strange complex with no friends. The first friend I made, Carlos, wanted to be more than friends. At first, I resisted. I had two young children. I was tired all the time. I had to focus on finding a daycare and a job. Besides, Frankie and I were still legally married. But Carlos persisted.

I was broke, so my only option was to pursue a divorce through legal aid. I filled out the paperwork and waited. It was legal aid, so it was going to be a long wait.

Loneliness and rejection will do funny things to a person's will. Soon, I started rationalizing. Well, I don't have my husband anymore, but I'm not dead. I'm nineteen. I do need to get back out there and start dating. I have no one else helping me. Frankie and I were together before we were legally married, too. Besides, Carlos is good to me and good with the kids...

When Frankie found out that Carlos and I started dating, his behavior changed. He started coming around more. He started talking about spending more time with the kids. He started talking about getting back together. But all I could think of were those words: "You're too ghetto..." I didn't see anything changing that. I didn't see anything, at all, changing for the better in our relationship. I did see Carlos being kind and attentive. I did see my kids happy with all of us together. Frankie stopped coming around.

One day, Frankie came to visit the kids and wanted to take them with him. Carlos tried to stop him. But Frankie was prepared. He had brought his brother with him and his brother threw Carlos up against the wall and pinned him while Frankie rushed the kids out of the apartment and into his car. He and his brother disappeared with the kids. I had no idea where they had gone.

I went to the police to report my kids being taken. "Look, miss," the officer said, "He's their father. His name is on the birth certificates. You're still legally married. There's nothing we can do."

There's nothing we can do.

Meanwhile, Frankie had gotten a lawyer, and soon, we were in court. He was suing for custody. I didn't have money to pay for a lawyer, but surely a judge wouldn't look kindly on a father who would just snatch up a toddler and a preschooler and take them away from their mother. I told the judge how Frankie had disappeared with my kids and I didn't know where they were. His lawyer argued that the fact that I was with someone else was worse.

"Your honor, she picked a man over her own kids. And, technically, my client had visitation rights and wasn't doing anything wrong."

"But, your honor! He won't give them back. He won't let me see them at all! He kidnapped them."

"Your honor, the law is clear in this case. The defendant is still married to my client. She's in an adulterous relationship. We move for primary custody."

The judge agreed. Frankie was granted primary custody of my one-year-old daughter and three-year-old son. I wouldn't be able to see them every day. I could only see them a few days a month. I left the courtroom and walked across the street to a park. I sat on a bench and cried. What I wouldn't have done to have a lawyer to defend me, to stand up and say that the loneliness had gotten to me—I had needed help and Carlos had been there—but that I was a good mom who loved her babies, that they needed me and they were too young to be without me.

Words from what seemed like a past life echoed on the wind in that park:

...And let none deal treacherously with the wife of his youth...

The thoughts rattled through my head for a full fifteen minutes as I sobbed out loud.

We had been so young. I had been put out by my own family. What was I supposed to do?

God, where are you?

Why is Frankie doing this? Doesn't he know how cruel this is? What am I supposed to do next? God, where are you?

Chapter 3

Living a Legacy

If God gives you something you can do, why in God's
name wouldn't you do it?
—Stephen King

I spent many years paying for my past and making up for it. My
younger years showed me how, no matter how someone has
been raised or how bright their future looks from a young age,
life can change in an instant. One conversation, one decision, one
person who has a little more power than you in a moment, can alter
your life. That promising future can disappear. All hope can vanish.
And despair is waiting around the corner to creep into your life and
overcome you.

I know what it's to sleep in a car, to be hungry, to endure
domestic violence, and to have my children taken away. Many
years later, I have vowed that, if I can ever help someone go through
that experience and come out the other side, I will. If I can help
someone avoid deep trauma, I will. If I can help someone turn

things around so that they can have hope once more, I will. I must do that. Because I know what it's like.

And, because—by the grace of God—I have come through the other side, and I can.

All my life, I've always helped everyone. They come to me. Sometimes, they want help when I've got nothing to give. And sometimes, they come to me with things I can't even help them with.

One of the wisest people I know is my grandma, my *abuela*. My father's mother, she raised the man who was compassionate enough to take in and care for a woman (my mother) and her young daughters after their father ran off with another woman. He cared for all of us like we were his own. He cared for my mother through her bi-polar disorder, her depression, and her manic episodes. Through it all, he loved her anyway.

His mother, my *abuela,* is as kind and generous as her son. There was no crisis I was going through that I couldn't bring to her. She always made time to listen. She has always reached out her hand to touch mine and comfort me when I have been hurting or frustrated.

It's in your DNA.
It's your calling.

In 2003, I moved to Florida and moved in with her while I looked for a better direction for my life. I was still struggling to get back on track. Some of the people I had allowed into my life since I had been with Frankie had piled on the hurt.

"*Abuela,* I'm not helping nobody no more! They take advantage of me every time!"

"You will help them, Marisol. It's in your DNA. It's your calling."

She was right, of course. I was pursuing a career in social work because I wanted to help people. And it *was* in my DNA.

My grandmother was born and raised in Puerto Rico. A commonwealth of the U.S. for well over 100 years, Puerto Ricans have been US citizens since 1917. Governors had been appointed who weren't even from Puerto Rico. But that started to change in the mid-1940s, and when Puerto Rico created her constitution, the people were finally able to democratically elect their own governor in 1948.

In 1949, Luis Muñoz Marín took office. The commonwealth had just gone through a time of great political upheaval after a devastating hurricane had taken out the sugar crop and left much of the island unemployed while also facing overcrowding.

During his previous decade in the Puerto Rican senate, Muñoz Marín had proposed housing projects, education loans, and free clinics. A former writer and journalist, he was well aware of the plight of the Puerto Rican people and has since been regarded as the "Architect of the Puerto Rico Commonwealth." He desperately sought political, social, and economic reforms for Puerto Rico and her people and was not afraid to make decisions to achieve those goals.

When my *abuela* was a young woman, her passion for helping others led her to be a social worker. In this new commonwealth, there were many problems and a great deal of poverty to address. As a social worker, she was called on to visit with and assess the condition of families in various communities. Conditions were pretty bad. In the early 1950s, people began fleeing for the United States. Over the next twenty years, Puerto Rico would lose 25% of its population to La Gran Migración (The Grand Migration). But those left behind needed help. And my *abuela* was determined to help them.

In 1965, Roberto Sánchez Vilella, handpicked by Muñoz Marín, became the new Governor. But party politics upset his re-election bid and Luis A. Ferré was elected the following term. An engineer and industrialist, his governorship focused on economic growth. But he had a deep concern for the young people in Puerto Rico. He lowered the voting age and appointed young adults to high-level positions. He had a particular interest in services supporting young people and their families.

At the time, my grandmother's job was assessing the welfare of these struggling families. However, merely assessing their situation wasn't enough for my *abuela*. When she saw that a family was hungry, she brought them food. When she talked to a little boy with holes in his shoes, she found someone with shoes to give to him. When she had to duck under a roof that was falling down on a family, she made sure that someone was going to visit that home with the tools to fix it. Over time, the governor heard about the woman who was solving crisis after crisis in families around Puerto Rico.

"Did you know the governor, *abuela*?"

"Of course, *niña*."

"What did he say to you?" "He said I could have his stamp. And I was so happy. I knew it meant I could help more people!"

In those days, when you had the "stamp" of a government official, it meant that you had tacit permission to make decisions and represent government interests. The governor's stamp effectively granted *Abuela* access to *all* of Puerto Rico's resources. It was an honor. But for my *abuela*, it was an answer to prayer and an opportunity to do more for her people.

For my *abuela*, serving people wasn't merely her profession. It was her life. At home, she nursed her bedridden husband through his illnesses before setting about her day serving the community. When she got home, she cooked, cleaned, and nursed her husband and children some more. Her work was never done. She never got a day off. It was not only expected, it was in her heart to do everything she could for those around her. It was her calling.

After a career in social work, *Abuela* moved to the U.S. with her family. She settled in Massachusetts and started a childcare program. She was ready to follow rules and regulations, just as she had in Puerto Rico. But, establishing childcare in a different state brought a whole new learning curve to starting a business entity. When I started my non-profit, she was a font of information.

"First, you have to pick a name. What do you want to call it?"

"I don't know, *Abuela*. I have to pray about that. It needs to be personal because I want to personally help people, like you did. I understand the path they're on. I've been there, too, so I can be a kind of guide for them as they walk that path..."

"Okay. So, what are you going to do for the people?"
"I don't know all of that, yet. I think I have to incorporate first and get a tax ID number and non-profit status."

"Yes, but you need to find a location that's good with a building that will pass inspection..."

"A building? I can't do that now! I don't even know what that will cost."

"Well," Abela said, "Find out. You can do it. I know you can do it."

So, I did. I incorporated Guided Path and pursued non-profit status. With my *abuela's* guidance, I started searching for grants. After some time, leg work, and God's favor, we were in business. When tax time came, I sat down with my accountant for the first time.

"So, how are you paying rent on this building if you haven't had any donations, yet?"

I grinned apologetically. "Well, I kind of gave up my apartment."

"Wait, so you're staying in the building?"

"Yes, but it has plumbing and a sink. And we have been pursuing grants, so I know it's temporary."

"But how are you feeding the people who come to you for food?"

"Usually, my paycheck from my day job. But I'm starting to see some local businesses helping, too. And I have a relative who is an architect and working on plans for a better facility."

"How long have you been in business?"

"Six months."

"Only six months? And you already have non-profit status? I've been in business for forty years and I've never seen that. I know established churches that are still waiting on their official non-profit status. How in the world did you get that done so fast?"

I shrugged, "God's favor, I guess."

There were trials behind me and ahead of me, but I did feel God's favor on me. He had given me a grandmother who had shared the love that I was looking for—the love that was pulled away from me at fourteen when I was told to leave home. I faced twenty years of hardship and heartache from that point on. If *Abuela* hadn't taken me in back in 2003 for a whole year when I needed her most, if she hadn't guided me, talked to me, encouraged me, and mentored me, I wouldn't have been able to make the changes in my life that I needed to make.

More importantly, if my grandmother hadn't poured into me, then I wouldn't have gotten the education, knowledge, and resources I needed in order to pour into others. Her love and wisdom guided me away from my own brokenness so that I could live a life of benevolence. When I see people walk into our building, I see the deep creases in their foreheads. I see the clothes that need to be washed. I hear the familiar sound of feet dragging on the floor in hopeless desperation.

I also see their warm smiles as I offer to fill their coffee cups. I hear them sigh contentedly as they lean back in a chair and, maybe for the first time that week, look up to watch a TV show after a filling meal. I hear the sound of hope creep into their voices as they chat excitedly with our volunteers because they finally got that check in the mail they had been waiting on for so long. I feel them squeeze my hand as they tell me about the thing that happened to them, that disruptor, that trauma, that led them to be so down and out.

And, I feel my *abuela's* hand squeezing back.

Chapter 4

Birthing a Dream

Change is inevitable. Growth is optional.
—John Maxwell

I was sitting in my room at my *abuela's* house, doing my homework. I had finally gone back to school and earned my associate's degree in human services. Now I was on track to get my bachelor's in social work. As a social work case manager, I would be called on to help families in need, and it wasn't that long ago that *I* was one of those families.

It was August 2009, and it had been an emotional time. I was single, and my youngest child was with me. I tried not to spend my time thinking about why my older three weren't there, as once I fell into that dark hole, it took a while for me to crawl back out. And things were finally getting better. I had to stay on track for the sake of my youngest—and for my sanity.

I took a break from studying and continued my research on what it would take to create a successful nonprofit. I had been entertaining that dream for a while and I wanted to do the work to create it. I already had a lot on my plate since I was working my way through school, but I was determined to build it. I saw my future as a social worker pretty clearly. I wanted to always be helping people, but instead I found myself always doing paperwork.

Nestled in the safety of *Abuela's* home, I was able to focus on the changes I needed to make to get my own life fully back on track. I had needed a change in scenery. I had needed to stop seeing my boyfriend. I had been working paycheck to paycheck, so every minor financial setback became a major crisis.

Abuela knew that what I needed was a stepping stone to a new beginning. She could be that stepping stone, so she offered to take me in. What I was learning was that every time you step up and cross a stepping stone to pass a level in life, you're building more stepping stones as you go. Each step leads to the next. And once you get started, each step seems easier.

A few years before, in the midst of the worst heartache and despair of my life, the first stepping stone didn't seem possible, much less reachable. After I left Frankie, I found work, and I had not been without work since. But, with no safety net, we would find ourselves with no food, or, if it was a big enough rough patch, living in my car. Sometimes, I was too proud to ask for help. But I often felt like I was on the verge of things getting slightly better (where I wouldn't need help) or slightly worse. Mostly, I was doing my best to adult and was just not very good at it.

My *abuela* walked by the open door and poked her head through the doorway.

"Marisol, are you still studying? It's late."

"I know, *Abuela*. I'm researching about creating my non-profit. There's so much to do. Sometimes, I wonder if I'm the one who is supposed to be doing this."

Abuela sat on my bed. "*Mi cariña*, if not you, then who?"

"But *Abuela*, I'm only just getting back on my feet. I just wonder if it's the right time."

She laughed. "What you're doing is like having a baby. If you wait for the perfect time, the baby will never come."

I laid my head in my hand and sighed, but *Abuela* wasn't finished.

"Marisol," she looked at me firmly, her dark eyes flashed in the lamplight. "There's so much more to you than you know. There's something special about you. You have the heart, and the intelligence, and the passion. Your wrong choices put you in a bad place. If you're done with the wrong choices, then you're ready."

Tears sprang to my eyes under the hard truth within her tender words. I *was* done. I knew what was right. I had been taught well. I had just given in to fear, loneliness, and desperation. But, the same people who taught me what was right also taught me that there is a God who forgives. I had sought His forgiveness, so there was nothing more I could do to correct my errors or alleviate the pain I still carried. I had done all I could. The rest was up to God. My future was in His hands.

I had done all I could. The rest was up to God.

I set to work right away to set up the legal documents and I officially launched. I knew that, realistically, I would have to take my time to develop the organization. I was a single mom working and going to school. There was only so much time in the day to operate a fully-functioning human services charity. I couldn't afford to hire help. I was too new to have volunteers. So, I started the slow and steady work of building a non-profit business.

A few years in, I had to take a break and prioritize school and family. While I was regrouping, I met my second husband. He appreciated that I had a good job and took care of my family, and he was eager to support me. I let him know that my heart and my calling was to return to building Guided Path as soon as I was able. He assured me that he would support me then, too.

In 2018, I was ready, but my husband wasn't. He couldn't understand why I would quit a good paying job with benefits to help other people.

"Because I've been there. I know what it's like to be desperate and alone."

"Other people know what that's like, too, but they don't quit their jobs once they get one."

"But this is what I've been building and working toward. It's why I made the professional and academic decisions I've made. Everything has led to this."

"You have a good paying job at a hospital with great benefits. A great family. Isn't that enough for you?"

I shook my head. "This has nothing to do with me. It has to do with helping the people who need it."

He shot back, "Well, right now, I'm the one who needs help. I need you to keep your job."

"But your paycheck is actually enough for us to live on. And, I told you when we got together that I had started a non-profit and, as soon as I could, I was going to relaunch it."

"Marisol, I forbid you to quit your job. Forget about that non-profit."

"You *forbid* me? You forbid me to give up everything I've worked toward? You forbid me to give up my calling?"

I was heartbroken. A man who had seemed to care so much and support my dreams was now turning out to be all talk. It now sounded like he supported me as long as it didn't impact his ability to spend my money.

"Yes, I forbid it. You need to drop the subject. If you don't drop it, if you quit your job, I'm gone. It's either your non-profit, or me."

I looked at him, seeing him for the first time. I had been so clear with him from the time we met. I felt betrayed. I felt cheated. All of those times that he said he supported my goals, he was just telling me what he thought I wanted to hear. Had he ever taken me seriously? Did he think I'd just forget about my calling?

But my husband's threats drove fear into my heart—fear of being single again. It was already a risk to consider living on one income, but could I grow a non-profit without him? I could get a part-time job, maybe, but could I live on that? I had a 401K, but that would only keep me going for about six months. What could I do? People worse off than me needed my help, but I was scared.

I remembered Esther, the Queen of Persia who had an opportunity to save her people. The king had given an order to put a group of people to death. What he didn't know was that they were Esther's people. Her Uncle Mordecai found out and told Esther. But Esther was reluctant to speak up. If she spoke out of turn in the king's presence, he might get angry and have her put to death. When the time came for her to act, she hesitated. Afraid for her life, she argued with her uncle. But Mordecai, her mentor as well as her uncle, talked her through it: "...who knows whether you have come to your position in the kingdom for such a time as this?"

Esther had been called to help people, and God had arranged events so that she could have the opportunity to help by placing her in the right place at the right time. It could have cost her her life, but she did it anyway, she approached the king, unbidden. Now it was time for me to be brave, like Esther.

I was devastated at the thought of losing my marriage. But I had been through greater loss. And if I could survive that, I could survive anything.

I called my *abuela* and told her what was happening. If I decided to move forward, I needed to make sure I was being realistic. She said, "Keep going!"

I relaunched in 2018. I was single again, but I was determined to fulfil on what I felt God had called me to do. He had sustained me. He had prepared me. I was ready.

I started researching properties. I found a 2,800 square-foot building for rent on Waters Avenue in Tampa, with a bus stop right out front. There were two warehouses adjacent to the property, so the lot was a good size. It was perfect. I told the leasing agent that my timeline was based on the grants I had applied for. The leasing agent was familiar with the grant-writing process. He knew it might be a bit of a wait, so he gave me the space rent-free for a year. All he asked for was the deposit.

Since we reopened, we've operated for three years without almost any funding. Many miracles made that happen. Other organizations, both public and private, have found out what we are doing and have offered to share their resources with us. Restaurants and grocery stores have donated food. Local programs use our location as a distribution point. The Florida Board of Health partners with us to offer HIV and Hepatitis C testing. I sit on planning and outreach committees that serve the homeless population. Through good, strong partnerships, God has opened doors all over the city.

Today, we provide a hot meal Monday through Friday for anyone who comes. They can have two meals a day. In between, they are invited to sit inside and cool off in the air conditioning. They can watch TV and have as much coffee and water as they like. They can stay as long as they want. Every Sunday, we offer food distribution. We see struggling families and working people who are barely making ends meet. When they run out of peanut butter or milk, they don't have to go hungry. We can help.

And our future is very, very bright. In 2022, we are scheduled to break ground on a 25,000 square foot emergency shelter and multi-purpose facility. It will house our services and provide a place for families and individuals in crisis. It will have a chapel and a full kitchen. After operating for almost a decade with no funding, God has used partnerships and the people of our community to make miracles happen.

Our volunteers have been the lynchpin to our growth and are the reason we are where we are today. Because of them, we are not only able to deliver help to people, but we can deliver the help that people truly need. But, that's a story for them to share in the next chapter.

Chapter 5

The Path Guides

We make a living by what we get,
we make a life by what we give."
—Winston Churchill

The room is spacious with a half-dozen round tables set up in the center and a TV high overhead on the wall. Several people are sitting at the tables looking up at the TV, some eating off of styrofoam plates, some sipping coffee.

As the TV hums, excited chatter is coming from the volunteers in the back of the room. An unexpected food donation had just arrived, and plans needed to be made for its distribution.

A professionally-dressed man grins and shakes his head. "I can't believe this. And gifts for kids, too. Totally unexpected. We're going to have to figure out a way to hand these out." He examines the gifts. He lifts a box holding a doll and sees an art kit underneath. "These kids are going to be so happy."

"Parents, too. Most of them can't afford gifts for their kids." A woman with short gray hair and a clipboard steps forward. "You know, we can hand these out with the food. Same event."

The man nods. "Yeah, parents are going to need these soon." He turns to the volunteers. "This is going to give hope to so many families." The small group nods in agreement.

The woman with the clipboard bustles about the pile of toys. "We need to account for every donation. We can't leave anything out." She starts writing on the clipboard.

Marisol emerges from the kitchen with another aluminum foil pan. The steaming rice was cooked in her kitchen at home the night before, along with the beans and chicken. She sets it out on the counter with the other dishes and rushes back to the kitchen where a man in jeans and a plaid shirt is stirring more beans on the stove. He looks up as a new volunteer enters behind Marisol. "It's new!" he points to the various appliances, the cooler next to him, and the stove where his pot sits, simmering. He smiles warmly and nods at the new volunteer.

Marisol laughs and says, "That's right. A restaurant sold us some of this equipment and they hardly asked anything for it. We needed it so badly. It's so amazing!"

"New!" the man grins, nodding.

"He doesn't speak much English, sorry," Marisol apologizes and sees the volunteer examining multiple industrial shelves stacked with food.

"That's for our food distribution," she says, pointing to the shelves. "We hand out food every Sunday. We get donations for some of this food, too," She nods at the stove. "But, whatever we don't have, I buy. I work part-time a few days a week, so whatever I can do to make sure I have enough food, I do."

The man stirs the beans and smiles at Marisol in apparent understanding.

"I'm just praying that this seasonal job I have now lasts a bit longer. There's always something we need. Not to mention that I have my own bills to pay!" She laughs. "But God seems to provide the miracles it takes to keep us going."

Marisol hurries out of the kitchen with another large pan of food covered in foil and leads the new volunteer to the long bar outside the kitchen covered in foil dishes. "I get home at about eight or nine o'clock in the evening and start cooking. Then I refrigerate it and get up at five a.m. to get it all ready." She smiles and looks up. "It's a long day."

She walks around the bar to the pile of toys stacked against the half wall. "Have you met Daisy? She's been with me a long time."

The woman with the clipboard looks up and smiles. "Yes, I have. When I met Marisol, we were both working at the hospital. When she told me about her plans for Guided Path, I thought, 'Wow, she is exactly the person to do this.'" Daisy lowered her clipboard and stepped closer, "Have you heard her story? What she's been through? Well, if you had, then you'd know why she's doing this."

Daisy sets her clipboard on the bar. "It was wild. Here's this woman who's working with me at the hospital, helping people get the assistance they need to pay their medical bills. She's a social worker. She's got a good job. When she tells me what she wants to do, I think she's crazy. I know she's good at helping people, but what she wants to do is huge. How is she going to do it?" Daisy said, looking at Marisol.

Marisol smiles and shrugs. Daisy continues. "And then she told me her story. She's been where these people are." Daisy nods to the center of the room. "She totally understands what they're going through. More importantly, as a social worker, she knows how to help them." Daisy grabs her clipboard. "And she knows what needs to be done with stuff like this." She nods to the pile of toys.

She's been where these people are

Marisol chimes in, "Yeah, every donation we get, whether it's food or something else, it needs to be logged. There's a lot of paperwork. That's one of the reasons I have to spend so much time here, even with great volunteers like Daisy who can totally handle so much of what we do. But everything needs to be accounted for, there are grants that need to be applied for, local people who want to meet me and see what we're doing. I have another job, but I'm here all the time."

Daisy nods, "Yep."

Marisol looks around the room, "Have you met Tecaira? I think she's in the office."

They walk back towards the storefront window steering around the tables. Marisol walks through the office door, past file cabinets towering against the walls, and over to a large desk where a young woman sits. She looks up and smiles.

"Tecaira, this is our new volunteer. I wanted her to meet you."

Tecaira stands, smiling kindly. "Hi, I'm Tecaira. I'm a volunteer, too."

Marisol adds, "Tecaira came here to volunteer to fulfill on some volunteer hours for school. That was a few years back. She's helped a lot of people since then."

Tecaira smiles, her white teeth bright against her sable skin. "Yep. I'm still here. Marisol keeps me busy. There's always somebody to see." Her eyes flicker to the doorway toward the tables in the center room. "I sit with them and work with their cases. Whatever they need."

Tecaira sits back down in the chair. "I wish I had more time to give, but I get to come in a few hours in the mornings. There is always someone who needs some help calling the food stamp office because some paperwork got messed up, or they might need help looking for a job."

Marisol adds, "Yes. We do what we can with job placement. Sometimes, they just need some extra help. One of our clients was a regular and was actually starting to help out around here. He had applied for work, but no one would hire him because he had a history with drugs." Marisol sighed. "All he needed was someone to vouch for him. But we know the manager at the convenience store not far from here. He had applied there, but the manager wasn't sure about him—just wasn't sure he'd show up. But we had gotten to know this man and assured him that he would show. He just needed a chance."

Tecaira nods, "And he's still there. There are so many people who just need that kind of help. They need someone to make a call for them to the Medicaid office, someone who knows how to talk to the people there to get them the information they need. A lot of people can't work because they don't have ID. They lost it and they don't have access to a birth certificate or anything. Those things get lost. People move around, or their stuff gets stolen... Do you know how hard it is to get an ID when you don't have your paperwork?" Tecaira's voice changes pitch, her emotion showing. "Here they are, struggling through bad breakups, mental illness, overcoming addiction... and they can't prove who they are. It makes a normal life impossible." She pauses, allowing time for imagining what life would be like without basic, necessary documentation.

"It stops them from doing anything to get themselves out of crisis," Marisol says. "Without ID, they can't do anything."

"Well," Tecaira adds, "we help them with that. They can order new documentation and they can use our address to do it. That's all some of them need. Access to a computer and an address to get mail."

"The point is," Marisol says, "Tecaira sits with them until whatever their need is gets met. We never say no."

Tecaira laughs heartily. "That's right! That's what Marisol has taught me. No one is ever told no. We tell them, 'Let me see what I can do to help,' and then we do everything we can."

No one is ever told no.

"That's right," Marisol nods. "And we don't stop until we find a way to help. But just letting them know that we'll do whatever we can to help, just telling them that we'll try everything lets them know that they're worth helping. They need to know that. They need to have hope that, yes, today isn't good. What's going on right now isn't okay. But tomorrow things will be better. The only way to build that trust with them so that they can believe tomorrow will be better, so they can have the strength to get back on their feet, is to do everything we can to help them with whatever they're dealing with today."

Marisol looks back into the main room. "Let's go back out here. I want to introduce you to Bobbie."

The professionally-dressed man paused his conversation with the small group when he saw Marisol approaching. "Bobbie," she says, "I wanted to introduce you to our new volunteer. This is Bobbie. He was a Tampa police officer for thirty years. He comes from a family of officers. His brother is the former police chief. He's been a really important part of our growth. He really understands what we're trying to do here."

"Well," Bobbie's deep voice drawls, "It's not hard to see." He smiles at Marisol.

"I was on the force for thirty years." Bobbie continues, "I have a financial services business now. I wanted to do something that allowed me to have flexibility in my schedule to help with a place like this." Bobbie looks around the room. "Once you come here and see what's going on, how people are helped in real time and never turned away, never denied, you know what a difference this is making in people's lives."

"I come from an area of town where a lot of kids I grew up with ended up in a bad place. We were okay because our father was around and made sure we were okay. He didn't let us out on the street after dark. He made sure we weren't hanging out with a crowd that was going to land us in jail. But some of my friends weren't so lucky. They ended up in trouble. And once trouble starts, it follows you."

Bobbie glances toward the tables where several men and a few women sip coffee and scrape their plates with their forks. "As an officer, there was only so much I could do to help my friends. I knew they needed help. Some things I could do, but I couldn't do everything. There are programs with the city and programs with the county, but sometimes they have a hard time working well together, or their hands are tied, or the people behind the desk who want to help are told, "No, that's not our mission.""

"Bobbie is the president of our board of directors," Marisol adds. "He knows our mission well: do whatever it takes to get people access to the services they need."

Bobbie nods, "Yes, that's the key. So many people can't get through the red tape that other programs have. They can't get a 'yes,' even when they're doing everything they can to get the assistance they need. If they could just get a little help, most people could deal with whatever they're going through. That's the gap we fill. We give people what they need so they can solve their own problems."

We give people what they need so they can solve their own problems.

"It's the encouragement they need more than anything," Marisol adds. "It's that hope. It goes back to building up their strength. If I hadn't had my grandmother all those years when I had been beaten and beaten down, I wouldn't have had the strength. Not everyone is lucky enough to have a grandmother like mine, or people who have their back and who can keep them going when they've lost hope. Without that, anyone going through a tough time is going to spiral downward."

"If you talk to any of these people," she nods toward the tables, "they'll tell you. Many of them are professionals, had good jobs, had a good life. But then a crisis hit. One of our clients was an architect. He was doing fine. Then his girlfriend broke up with him. It was a really bad breakup. She might not have known it, but she broke him down completely. He couldn't get over it. It affected everything. He lost his job, his livelihood, then his house. From there, it didn't take long for him to become homeless. A lot of people like that end up here in Florida because the weather is good all year 'round and they can survive here. He's from up north. All he needed was another job and a way to get back up there. He could have done it on his own with one of the stimulus checks, but he didn't have an address it could be mailed to. We let him use ours."

"You'd be surprised at all the charities and programs that don't allow that." Bobbie adds.

"Yep. Well, we went online last week, and saw that the check is on its way. He should have it in the next day or two. He'll be fine."

I heard Marisol's story, and I knew she was the one who wouldn't stop until these folks got the help they needed.

"But there are a lot of people who aren't fine without that kind of help." Bobbie says. "That's why I got involved with Guided Path. I heard Marisol's story, and I knew she was the one who wouldn't stop until these folks got the help they needed. That's why she never says no."

Marisol turns to the new volunteer, "I haven't told you my full story—the *whole* story—have I?"

Chapter 6

A Reckoning

The abuse didn't make you strong. You overcame
it because you're already strong. Let's not give
abusers credit for making us strong.
—Vassilia Binensztok

"Frankie, Marisol is good people. Why are you doing this to her?"

After two years, Frankie's brother stepped in. With Frankie as the primary custodial parent, I had only been able to see our young children every other weekend. For two years, I couldn't fix their lunches or tuck them in except a few days a month. I missed early childhood milestones, coloring with them, taking them out to the park...

When I found out I was pregnant, I was encouraged. I was meant to be with Carlos. But even a new baby couldn't take away the longing I felt every waking moment for the babies I couldn't have with me. All the joy and elation that surrounds the miracle of a new child coming into the world, with parents who love him and each other, was clouded by the sadness and the mourning I felt for the children who were slipping away from me, growing up without me.

Carlos tried to help. He scraped together $1,000 for a lawyer to get us back in court. The lawyer was certain we should at least get joint custody. Because Frankie's brother had talked to him, Frankie didn't fight it.

But Frankie was still working out of St. Louis. In order to make joint custody happen, I either had to drive to and from St. Louis or meet Frankie halfway in Springfield. Soon, the excuses started.

"I don't have the gas money to get them to you this weekend,"

"That's okay, Frankie, I'll meet you in Springfield."

"I can't get to Springfield."

"Well, I'll figure out a way to come to you."

"Don't worry about it. We have plans, anyway. I'll bring them to you next weekend."

It's not that I didn't want my children to spend time with their father—far from it. I was determined that they would never be pawns in our relationship. But soon it was clear that Frankie was playing a bit of a psychological game. There was always a reason he couldn't bring them to me or meet me halfway, and the excuses started wearing thin.

Before long, Frankie wasn't letting me see them at all. I reached out to attorneys. No one wanted to take the case. Frankie was providing for them financially. Each attorney told me that in the case of joint custody, judges almost never side against the parent who financially provides, and it wasn't as though Frankie was unfit. Sure, he was playing psychological games with me over visitation, but that's not abuse. There was nothing to argue. A few attorneys offered to try—if I could come up with the $3,500 retainer.

Visitation had disappeared altogether, and the only time I could spend with my kids was over the phone. Carlos and I welcomed our second child, but nothing was filling the void of my longing to be with my first two. Over the years, I tried to reason with Frankie.

"Frankie, this isn't right. You know we have joint custody."

"Well, Marisol, you're going to have to take me back to court and prove it."

"You know I can't afford that. And the joint custody paperwork I had got lost in one of our moves. You're the only one who has that paperwork."

"Yeah, well, you have a new family now. I've already told the kids that you'd rather be with them."

"But that's not true! You know that's not true!"

"You have two new kids, Marisol. Go take care of them."

A few years after our younger son was born, however, Carlos started to become less attentive than he had been. He seemed distant. This wasn't like him. I knew something was wrong. Part of me didn't want to know what it might be, but I was so desperate to replace the love I felt I had lost at the age of fourteen. If my husband no longer loved me, I had to know.

I was so desperate to replace the love I felt I had lost at the age of fourteen

Soon, I became aware that Carlos was cheating on me. It was the ultimate betrayal. He had walked with me through the pain of watching my two older children being taken away from me. He had known my struggle as a young mom on public assistance, begging for help through legal aid. He knew that rejecting me as his wife, rejecting my love, was putting me out. I had been put out before. All the old, familiar pain was back.

Carlos and I had been together for ten years. Now, a single mom again at only 29, I was on my own with two children. I had sought out good jobs and worked full-time, but the paychecks never stretched far enough. Because I worked full-time, I didn't qualify for public assistance. But I didn't make enough money to guarantee that there would be food in the house. I tried not to let my kids see how bad things were, but they were bad.

In 1997, my parents moved back to Puerto Rico. With only a sister in town who was living out her own drama, there was no one who could help me. When a financial blow hit, I had no choice but to send my kids to stay with their dad until it passed while I slept in my car. There is something about being on the verge of homelessness—and sometimes being homeless—that will convince you that you're not worth helping. I stopped asking for help. I stopped believing that I deserved it.

There is something about being on the verge of homelessness

Sometimes, I would find a man who would say all the right things to convince me that he would give me the love that I was so desperately searching for. It often turned out that, the better they were at convincing me, the worse they treated me. One day, a man had convinced a local pastor that he needed help. He just needed a leg up in the world. Even though my personal life was a train wreck, I had always had good jobs, so people assumed I was okay. The pastor reached out to me to help this man.

that will convince you that you're not worth helping

When the pastor introduced me to him, his tattered clothes told me the story of his hard life. He looked at me and smiled sheepishly. Sure, I said, I could help him. Soon, he talked me into going out with him. I had lost all discernment at this point in my life and accepted his advances. Maybe he would love me.

He didn't. But he did hit me. A lot. Whatever I said or did, it was an excuse to beat me. If I had the wrong expression on my face, I ended up on the floor. One day, I looked out the window and he didn't like that. He came across the room at me, pounced, and

I was soon a bloody, beaten mess, cut and bruised on the outside and torn apart, burned, and crushed on the inside. This time, even I couldn't ignore that I was the one who needed help.

even I couldn't ignore that I was the one who needed help

"*Abuela*, I don't know what to do."

"Marisol, if you don't leave *right now,* you are going to end up in a body bag."

"But I have nowhere to go."

"Yes, you do. You can come stay with me."

By 2003, my family had returned from Puerto Rico and relocated to Florida where my grandmother now lived. It was time to go. I had been fully torn down. I needed help to build back up.

"I'm coming, *Abuela*. Thank you. I love you."

"I love you, too, *mi corazón*."

I finally understood. It was my grandmother, all that time, who had the love for me that I thought I'd lost.

Chapter 7

Reconciled to a New Path

Youth fades; love droops; the leaves of friendship
fall; a mother's secret hope outlives them all.
—Oliver Wendell Holmes

Not everyone has an *abuela*, or a friend or family member, who can house them and offer emotional and practical support in a time of crisis. I was one of the lucky ones.

Before moving to Florida, when I was a bloody heap on the floor, feeling the physical and emotional torture of loneliness and longing, when I thought there was no way out—I am ashamed to admit it, but—I thought seriously about suicide. It shouldn't be a surprise, though. When you are that down, when your will has been broken over and over, when people with just a little bit of power over you seem to take away everything so that you're left with nothing to live for, that's where the mind goes. And I was certainly there.

My life back from the bottom wasn't easy. Even with my *abuela's* unfailing love and guidance, I still carry the scars of the beatings. Not the external ones, the *real* ones. I still feel like I have to be wary of trusting people because, in my search for love, I trusted too easily.

nothing hurt me more or cost me more than the time we were apart

And I still mourn for the time I lost with my older children that I'll never get back. There was trust that was broken there, too. They trusted that, once they were born, I would be the adult and not make childish decisions based on emotional needs. They trusted me to love them so powerfully that I would find a way to fight harder for them. They trusted that their dad, who they love and respect, would be honest and forthright with them, and not try to manipulate the situation in his favor.

One thing that they can trust, however, is that nothing I experienced in my life, no beating, no hungry or homeless nights, no loneliness or longing for love, nothing hurt me more or cost me more than the time we were apart. Nothing even comes close.

Today, I pray that they know how important they are and always will be to me. As adults, with clarity and a little bit of an explanation of things on my end, I think they know. They have both become adults that I am so proud and privileged to know. But the scars are still there, held together by the tenuous fibers of the trust we've built together since. My sweet daughter, who years ago became my best friend, had her trust in me challenged when I couldn't help a friend of hers. I had learned long ago that once someone deals outside of truth and takes advantage of good intentions, I have to stop helping. There is a point that, to remain safe in interpersonal relationships, we do have to say no. I pray that one day she will understand and become my best friend again. I miss her terribly.

So, even when life gets better, we can't cover up all our scars. Sometimes, though, our scars are a powerful reminder of what's important and what's right. My mission is to work toward a new day, a change in each community, each home, and each heart.

Chapter 8

The Future is Yours

Hope sees the invisible, feels the intangible, and achieves the impossible."
—Helen Keller

What would life be like if we could meet the needs of people in crisis and empower them to pull off their chains of despair?

The young woman at the reception desk who always seems distracted, touching up her makeup and pulling her bangs over her eyes, looks up at you today and cheerily asks, "Is there anything I can get you today?" She bounces up from her chair, whatever chip on her shoulder or weight she had been carrying is gone. She was rude to you last week and snapped at you for something, but today, it seems like she's a completely new person.

What you didn't know is that for the past three months she had been living in her car with her two young children, going to work fearful every day that one of them might spill the beans about their situation to a daycare worker and they'd be taken from her. Sometimes, tears would spill down her cheeks when she was alone at her desk and her makeup would run and her eyes would swell. She couldn't cover up her fear like she could cover up her makeup. But today, she is in a new apartment. For the first time in a long time, she is free from fear.

she is free from fear

And the new guy who works in the warehouse? Today he's at work, on time, and ready to go. He's started filling the orders already, and within thirty minutes he's ahead of schedule. Every delivery today is going to go out on time. Every customer is going to receive their product as expected, and every order will be accurately filled. There will be no angry customers at the end of the day, and they will all order again next month.

What you couldn't have known is that he's been hiding an alcohol problem. Every night, he tossed and turned, fighting for sleep, until he got out of bed and poured himself a drink. And another. And then another, until he fell asleep. The demons from his past had overtaken him, and to stop their rebuke, he was self-medicating. He'd roll off the couch in the morning, barely aware of where he was, and stumble into work

He's back in control of his mind

with no focus, no drive, and not caring. Today, he is sober and receiving the mental health services he needs. He's back in control of his mind and his life.

And you... what about you? If you walk past a man in the parking lot of the store in a wheelchair asking for spare change, what do you do? Do you look at him, see his thin frame and his amputated legs, fish around in your pocket for change, realize you don't carry any, and make a broad path around him to the other door? Do you walk up and down the aisles, wondering if he's hungry, wondering if you should buy him some peanut butter, some tuna... then it occurs to you—does he even want food? Would he be insulted if you offered? Is he hungry? What *does* he need?

What if you could walk up to him and say, "Hey, I know we don't know each other, but if you're hungry I know a place you can go. They'll feed you. They won't *They'll never* ask you to leave. They'll give you *turn you away* coffee. They'll talk to you. They'll make sure you're getting the services you need. And, if you're ever out here in bad weather, they're building an emergency shelter for people. You can go there. They'll never turn you away."

What if you could be the person who changed his life?

What kind of world do you want to live in?

Epilogue

Two men walk through the door, and the one I recognize speaks to me.

"Hi, Marisol. You may not remember me. You guys helped me a few weeks ago. I want to introduce you to a friend. His name is Alex."

Alex shakes my hand, and we find a table.

"Alex lost his ID, but everything he needs to replace it is back in Puerto Rico. Can you help him? He doesn't speak much English."

I turn to Alex and, in Spanish, I say, "Of course. We help people in your situation all the time, Alex. I'm going to go start a file for you."

A few weeks later, the two men return. Alex, still quiet, takes the envelope with his documents. "Thank you so much, Marisol," says the friend. "I knew you could help."

"No problem," I smile, "But you'll have to excuse me. I'm in a bit of a hurry, today. My *abuela* has come down with pneumonia, and I'm supposed to go to the hospital to visit her."

"Oh!" says the friend. "Is she okay? We know how important she is to you. Do you want us to go with you? "

I think this is a bit odd, but not unusual for the clients to show their gratitude with helpfulness.

"Sure, you're welcome to come with me."

At the hospital, Alex and his friend follow me into *Abuela's* room. I lean over and kiss my grandmother.

"How are you feeling, *Abuela*?"

"Much better, now that you're here, Marisol," she says brightly. "Who are these two gentlemen?"

"Oh, these are my friends."

Abuela pulls me close to whisper, "Well, that one looks like he likes you." She points to Alex.

I suddenly feel flushed. "*Abuela*, I only just met him! He's hardly spoken to me."

"Well," *Abuela* says knowingly, "I am hearing wedding bells."

"*Abuela*!" I whisper, feeling the heat on my face increasing. "That's crazy!"

Abuela smiles, "And I think he'll help you, too. If he's going to be your husband, he should help you at Guided Path. You do need someone to help you in the kitchen."

I look up at Alex in his jeans and plaid shirt and Alex looks back at me, smiling with fierce intensity. Suddenly, my future seems much brighter, and even more full of love.

GUIDEBOOK

for a new and better path

*E*veryone embarking on a new path needs a guide. And, for those who are called to make a difference for others, we are offering a guidebook so you can be deliberate in your walk and, in time, guide others.

Only you know your calling. You may be called to serve those who are in crisis, inspire those who need to be uplifted, assist those already engaged in acts of benevolence, or lead your community into a new way of being.

The pages that follow are intended to instruct and assist you as you move forward into your personal calling. It is merely a guide. Only you can put in the work. But, as the proverb says, "Whoever brings blessing will be enriched, and one who waters will himself be watered." (Prov. 11:25)

So, we invite you to open the Guidebook and see how you can bring a blessing to your community.

Identifying Your Calling

Your "Why"

The first step on the path to benevolence is identifying why you might be called to make a difference. The following pages include questions to get you started. There are no right or wrong answers. You will have an opportunity to write down your thoughts and reflections after each so you can return to these pages whenever you need a reminder of your "why."

1.   Have you ever gone through a personal crisis or trauma where you needed help?

   a. If so, who helped you?

   b. How did they help?

   c. How long did it take you to work through your crisis or trauma?

   d. Are you still struggling with the aftermath of your crisis or trauma?

Write your thoughts and reflections here (Try to include details that will remind you of what it feels like to need help):

Your Reaction to Others' Needs

The next step is to identify how you intuitively react to the needs of others. Are you quick to help? Do you need to think about it? Do you wonder how you can best help? Here are some questions to guide you:

1.   When someone I know opens up to me about a problem they are having and that problem is actually rather serious, what do I do?

    e.   Do I try to offer the best advice I can?

    f.   Do I try to think of a way that I, personally, can help them?

    g.   Do I try to think of someone I know who might be able to solve their problem?

    h.   Do I reach out to someone on their behalf and ask for help?

    i.   Do I point them to a resource or organization that may be able to help?

    j.   How do I feel when they share their struggle with me?

Write your thoughts and reflections here:

2.   When I see someone I don't know asking for help, how do I react?

a.   Do I try to avoid them because, when they ask, I'm not usually in a position to help?

b.   Do I try to evaluate whether or not they need the help?

c.   Do I do what I can to give them what they're asking for, hoping it will help them?

d.   Do I talk to them and try to find out more about their need?

e.   Do I offer to reach out to someone or an organization on their behalf?

f.   How do I feel when someone I don't know asks me for help?

Write your thoughts and reflections here:

Your Gifts and Talents

Many people find that using gifts and talents they already have makes helping others feel more natural and allows them to help more powerfully. Here are some questions to help you identify what area of benevolence you might be called to do:

1.   In my daily life, what do I already love to do?

     a.   Do I love to feed people (cook for them, see them enjoy food)?

     b.   Do I instinctively offer hugs when someone seems down?

     c.   Do I love to pray with people?

     d.   Do I enjoy talking to people, sharing words of encouragement?

     e.   Do I want to help people get organized and get details in order?

     f.   Do I freely share advice or strategies to help them with problems?

     g.   Do I love to do home improvement or yard projects?

     h.   Do I ask what they need in the moment and try to help with whatever it is?

Write your thoughts and reflections here (Include experiences that you may have had helping someone that especially gave you joy):

2. What have other people told me I'm particularly good at, or what have I done for people that they told me really helped them? Am I good at:

a. Talking people through their problems?

b. Showing lovingkindness or emotional support?

c. Jumping in and helping when others didn't?

d. Offering financial help?

e. Giving people practical information or tools to help them?

f. Saying the right thing at the right time to make someone feel better?

g. Sitting with people and helping them work through or think through their challenge?

h. Showing people what they need to do to resolve their issue?

i. Advocating for someone to get them the help they need?

Write your thoughts and reflections here (Include thoughts on how it made you feel to help someone in the way you helped them):

Finding Your Personal Guide

Who has helped you?

In order to help others, we must make sure that we, ourselves, have been helped and guided through life's challenges. Our ability to help others is attached to how well we've been mentored ourselves. Here are some questions to help you identify who has mentored you:

1.   Has anyone mentored me in my life?

a.   Were one or both of my parents available to me when I needed them?

b.   When I was a child, was there an adult who took time with me to help guide me through life?

c.   If so, who (could be more than one)?

d.   When I was a teenager, was there an adult who took time with me to guide me into adulthood?

e.   Do I feel like I adult pretty well now?

f.   When I'm struggling through a problem, do I have someone in my life who will drop everything and help me?

g.   Do I have someone in my life who has taken their own personal time to teach, train, or professionally guide me?

Write your thoughts and reflections here (Include some experiences that you may have had being mentored):

Identifying Your Mentor

If you are going to be someone who others can lean on, then you must have someone in your life that you can lean on. In the following pages, we provide a bonus chapter to help you identify and choose a mentor.

Before we begin, make a list of ten people you know and admire who you think might make a great mentor:

1.

2.

3.

4.

5.

6.

7.

8.

9.

10.

Mentorship

A lot of people have gone further than they thought they could because someone else thought they could. – Zig Ziglar

When you hear of people doing extraordinary things, most of us say, "Wow, that's awesome! I wish I could do that."

But, when a mentor does something extraordinary, we think, "Wow, I hope they teach me to do that."

A lot of people talk about mentorship. They talk about famous people and people who have achieved great things. They know the names of a few people who have written some good books that have helped or taught or influenced people. People are actively looking for mentors. There is an unfilled need in our culture to connect with people of wisdom, share our lives with them, and partner with them to do great things.

I was blessed to have a grandmother who has been there for me any time I needed mentoring. Not everyone has an abuela in their family who offers ready access to the very wisdom we need. But there are a few things I hope you can learn from when it comes to finding a mentor.

The privilege of access

Families who hand down a legacy of success might not realize the gift they are giving to their children and grandchildren. They give their children a front-row seat where they can observe and model the characteristics of a successful person.

Back in August of 2016, Time magazine published a piece on "Superfamilies." It gave insight into what different families do to create success. The story focuses on "super siblings." The author makes a strong case that, because all siblings in these families have achieved extraordinary success in different industries, there must be something they received in common at home during their formative years that laid the foundation for that success.

The article is an overview of a study where candidates were carefully selected and represented a spectrum of backgrounds, ideologies, and cultures. There were things common to these families that you would expect: they all put a high priority on education and expected their children to go to college, and the parents were involved in their children's lives.

And, there were other commonalities that were interesting. Most families had at least one parent who was an immigrant, an educator, or both. Most families were politically active and had a strong morality base. But there are, literally, millions of families in this country where that's true. What's the factor that makes these families—and all of their children—so successful?

It boils down to the way their parents were involved in their children's lives. They didn't merely ask about their day and do the random homework check or attend PTA meetings. It was much more than that. They provided mentorship.

Parents had specific messages that they wanted to ingrain in their children. They thought about ways to introduce lessons on the subject and drive home their point. They integrated normal childhood experiences like allowances and chores with broad life lessons, like the family's needs come before the individual's and we must be bold in our work ethic. Every parental and family decision was an opportunity to impart a meaningful lesson.

You know you're being mentored when you walk away from the interaction feeling stronger and wiser. You feel empowered to do better, do more, and reach further. And most important of all, you walk away believing that you can.

My abuela never stopped telling me, "You can do it!" Like a lot of people, I had ideas about what I should do. I had hopes of what I would do. But it took a mentor to tell me that I could do what I was being called to do.

What to look for in a mentor

Entrepreneur magazine ran an article on the characteristics of successful people in June of 2018. The author lists five basic characteristics:

1. Aspiration
2. Drive
3. Willingness to learn
4. Patience
5. Discipline

Now, my abuela isn't famous, and she hasn't written nine bestselling business books about wealth and success. But, what she does have in abundance is all five of these character traits.

1. Aspiration

My grandmother aspired to see a better future for Puerto Rico. The wave of recent political reform ran alongside a new way of thinking. She held tight to her powerful ideals, forged in the solid spiritual understanding that she was called to love her neighbor, and those ideals never left her, even after she moved to the US. She aspired to see all her neighbors in her community prosper.

Since leaving Puerto Rico, Abuela has lived in Massachusetts and Florida. She felt led to lift up and serve people in every community and from every walk of life. Whether it was a father facing the crushing economic event that took his job away, a mother who struggled to care for her sick child, or a granddaughter like me, who just couldn't seem to get rid of the drama in her life, my grandmother's door was always open.

Abuela said, "God told me to never close my doors." She has single-handedly helped many thousands of people in Puerto Rico, Massachusetts, and Florida.

2.   Drive

My grandmother's clear goals were to be a blessing to her family and to others in the community. She worked tirelessly to do everything that she did. Upon reflection, she said that it was her faith that propelled her forward when life got tough. And it did get tough. My grandfather battled cancer, and later in life, Alzheimer's. She attended to his every need when he was home. During the ten years that he suffered his worst illness, five of those years were spent in the hospital where she was by his side.

Of course, love and duty combine to become a driving force. But my grandmother was also driven to reach out to others in extraordinary ways to take on other people's struggles. In addition to raising her own three children, she later adopted eight more. Three of her adopted children were HIV-positive. While she was operating her daycare in Massachusetts, she was voluntarily taking on the love and nurture of those who needed her most.

"As long as God gives me life and keeps my mind intact, I'm going to help," Abuela said. As of this writing, she is 99 years old, and even from a chair in her nursing home, she is still driven to help others, including helping me run a non-profit.

3.   Willingness to Learn

From the age of seven, Abuela was called by God to help others. From that day on, she had to stay vigilant and coachable so that she could learn what it took to serve others. When she was bringing food to families in Puerto Rico as a social worker, she petitioned the new Governor, Luis Ferré, to grant her an allowance. Because of her reputation, the governor not only did that, but he gave her his official stamp so that she could approve welfare checks for low-income families and better help them.

When Abuela shifted from social work in Puerto Rico to childcare in Massachusetts, she had to adapt quickly, not only to doing business in a different language, but according to different rules and regulations under the Massachusetts Department of Children and Families. She had to learn how to interact with this new group of people. There were inspectors and auditors to deal with.

For my grandmother, she knew the fate and welfare of children hung in the balance. She had to learn to operate under a new system and adapt to a new paradigm. And she did.

4. Patience

Raising children and caring for a sick spouse will teach anyone patience. And certainly, my grandmother has demonstrated patience throughout the years with the thousands she has helped. The reality is that, in the human services and non-profit world, nothing will test your patience to the degree that people will. They are stubborn, indifferent, frustrating, and often bursting with anger and hurt. They will act out, pound their fists, curse, snap at the very people trying to help them, and frankly, they can be quite abusive. In no arena is patience more needed than in human services.

I spent a year living with my grandmother because it took me that long to get back on my feet, mentally, emotionally, and spiritually. And, it took that long because of, well... me. My grandmother had been speaking wisdom to me every day, but it took me a year to really hear and understand it.

When people are in crisis, feeling desperate, or facing trauma, they don't listen or process very well. Communicating with people in these situations takes perseverance and longsuffering. There is no one I know who has been more patient with me than my abuela. And, an abundance of time and patience is what it took to give me the help I needed.

5. Discipline

There is a verse in the Book of Deuteronomy that talks about how we should deal with God's commandments: "You shall teach them diligently to your children, and shall talk of them when you sit in your house, when you walk by the way, when you lie down, and when you rise up..."

Being obedient to God's will takes tremendous discipline. It's something that needs to be done daily and continually throughout each day. The focus and discipline needed to remain obedient to impart godliness in our families trips up even the most seasoned believers.

Everything I know about the Bible I learned from either my stepfather or his mother, my abuela. She and my grandfather pastored a church in Puerto Rico, in addition to all her other areas of service to the family and community. To live that kind of life, to be that productive, that fruitful, and to see that fruit manifest in real knowledge and wisdom in your children, takes an extraordinary amount of discipline. I think we all aspire to have just a portion of that kind of discipline in our own lives.

You may have someone in your own life who has mentored you and helped guide you in various ways. I was blessed to have a single person model all five characteristics. Sometimes, it takes more than one mentor to find someone who can model all five traits. But, if they're successful in life, they most likely do have all five characteristics.

How to find a mentor

So, where are you in life? The mentor you had yesterday might not be the mentor you'll need tomorrow. Hopefully, you'll create a lasting relationship with someone you can count on to guide you through your daily drama for a long while. But, if you don't have anyone in your life you can depend on for that kind of help, you should probably look at where you are in your life right now and start there.

Are you focused mostly on your personal life? Your professional life? Both? Where is your community? Do you pretty much stay local, or do you interact with people worldwide? Identify where you are now and look for someone who may have been in a similar place as you within the last decade or two.

When looking for a mentor, make sure you are looking for someone you admire. If your life turned out like theirs, would you be happy? Would you be proud of your accomplishments? You don't want to seek out a successful person in your field to model and then find out that they have no character or integrity; that they're someone who, if you were to become more like them, would actually be pulling you backward.

Make sure that anyone who might be a potential mentor is ahead of you in all areas of growth: personal, mental, emotional, financial, and spiritual. People can't guide you forward if they spend most of their time behind you.

If you are particularly focused on your professional life right now, it makes sense to reach out to someone in your arena who is successful in a similar area. My grandmother's extraordinary gift to me is that everything she has had to teach me, whether modelling compassion or teaching me how to interact with a county inspector, had purpose and built me up.

If your focus is more personal, whether it be relationships or spiritual pursuits, look around within your community for someone of like mind who is living the kind of life you would love to live, yourself. There is probably much to learn from him or her.

Whether personal, professional, or both, success doesn't happen in a vacuum. You need someone—or maybe more than one someone—who can walk in front of you, someone who can point out pitfalls and protect you from harm, who can show you things you might have missed and help you see the beauty in your journey.

But most of all, you need someone, like my Abuela, who can walk alongside you when the journey is tiring and say, "Let's keep going. I know you can do it."

Who Needs Me?

Here are some questions to help you identify who needs your help and space to record your thoughts:

Who have I seen in my community who I've thought, "I wonder if they need help?" (If you know their names, list them here. If not, describe them or where you saw them.)

1.

2.

3.

4.

5.

6.

7.

8.

9.

10.

What are some organizations I know about that could use my support, financially or as a volunteer?

1.

2.

3.

4.

5.

What are some causes about which I'm passionate (e.g., homelessness, animal welfare, helping the hungry, children in crisis)?

1.

2.

3.

4.

5.

Creating Your Own Path

After you've looked around your community for organizations, programs, and services that help in the areas you are passionate about, you might find that there isn't an organization in your area to serve that segment of your community. If that's the case, and you are willing and able to make ample time to forge your own path, here are some resources to get you started:

Council of Nonprofits
https://www.councilofnonprofits.org/tools-resources/how-start-nonprofit

U.S. Small Business Administration
https://www.sba.gov/business-guide

Because you've joined us on our Guided Path, you are welcome to reach out to our organization for help.

An Invitation to Join Us on Our Path

Thank you for taking the time to journey with us this far. We invite you to continue to walk with us. If you feel a call to help others and you would like to link arms with us, we can find a place for you. We are so grateful for your heart and your help. Please know that, as we grow, we will never lose sight of our mission to help whom we can, any way we can.

We never say no to the people who ask for our help, and we will never say no to those who want to walk alongside us on this path to help others, one life at a time.

GuidedPathFoundation.org

May God bless you and keep you and make His face to shine upon you and grant you peace.

About the Author

*A*n advocate against and survivor of domestic abuse and homelessness, Marisol Sanchez, founder and CEO of Guided Path, originally founded the organization in 2009. The following year, Marisol put the establishment on hold while she completed her paralegal studies. Relaunched in 2018, Guided Path has provided hot meals, clothing, and Medicaid assistance to residents and community members of the Hillsborough County-Tampa area. She hopes to use her life experiences and passion to empower and guide others who have suffered similar experiences in improving their lives and outcomes.